Dearly Befuddled

by

Katherine Finstuen

with illustrations by
Jessica Lyman Finstuen

Dearly Befuddled

Copyright © 2022 by Katherine Finstuen
Published by Waterton Publishing Company
Crystal River Books
watertonpublishing.com
ISBN 978-1-7347632-8-7

All rights reserved. No part of this book may be reproduced, stored, or transmitted by any means whether auditory, graphic, mechanical, or electronic without written permission of the author, except in the case of brief excerpts used in critical articles and reviews. Unauthorized reproduction of any part of this work is illegal and is punishable by law.

Because of the dynamic nature of the Internet, any web addresses or links contained in this book may have changed since publication and may no longer be valid. The views expressed in this work are solely those of the author and do not necessarily reflect the views of the publisher, and the publisher hereby disclaims any responsibility for them.

The only thing that you absolutely have to know, is the location of the library.

Albert Einstein

Too many epigraphs may not exactly spoil the book, but such a lack of focus should inspire a warranted wariness in the reader.

Katherine Finstuen

for the libraries of my life

preface

Let's pretend I left readers wanting more, yearning to combat their darkness-heaped window panes, clouds slumping across the sky, with this author's own particular brand of sunshine, that which can nourish and lift spirits, though not entirely salubrious — illuminating this planet and its inhabitants with rays penetrating a decimated ozone layer. Yes, I thought. That's a nice pretend. But how to organize? I ponder as I step, for I am a walker. As some immerse themselves in their element with swimming, with running, with cycling, I find myself in measured strides. Among other fascinations my rambling brings with it glimpses of little free libraries of all dimensions and styles, whether gloriously stocked or plundered to a humbled and dwindled selection. Rarely do I pluck titles from within, but what if, I thought…what if I opened those miniature portals to find more singular, more personal emblems of my past? Nearly as powerful as scent in their ability to send me sojourning into the vast swath of jumbled memory, the shelves of my brain? I have imagined these little free libraries of the mind. Dearly befuddled, let us explore, selecting those items which entice, replacing others with a quiet click of the door.

face

I. reading frenzy

I read not quite constantly but nearly so. Avariciously. People intrude and I'd rather they didn't. Far less interesting are they and sometimes require small talk. Given my reclusive tendencies the pandemic affected me far less than most in many ways. But when access to the library became non-existent, then blessedly reopened though quite limited in both hours and stock, I struggled. I know, I know, if that comprised my biggest hardship, well: shut up. And admittedly, the dearth of library books prompted visits to my own shelves for available tales. I reread works unvisited for years. I dipped into my inherited set of Dickens. I read a book about mountain goats purchased 20 years prior due to my amusement at the title alone: *A Beast the Color of Winter*. I read a book about the Sierras by John Muir, reveling in his description of a windstorm experienced atop a tree. Given my love of books, of words, meandering slowly toward the path of authorship does not bewilder. It wilders. The trail beckons in its multitudes of language and story; finding an audience along the way necessitates another, more circuitous route, ill kempt and bepotholed, no Adopt-a-Highway marker sponsored by a benevolent donor in sight.

Venturing into the treacherous world of publishing an unagented, unsolicited manuscript of unsurpassed oddity, I knew I would be faced with rejection. I likened it to those stretches of road directly preceding a "Begin Scenic Route" sign. I always feel bad for the landscape located just before the message. What a major self-esteem deflator. And it's *always* there, a constant reminder for all to see (except the blind or illiterate) that *you*, yes *you* are so inferior to what comes next public funds have been dedicated to announce your deficiency. Others' works garlanded the land beyond, belonged there, but not my own.

All I've ever heard or read from authors regarding the process of submitting their work suggests the writer should expect to be buried beneath an avalanche of nos before a trowel capable of mighty deeds unearths (or unsnows) that author from a spurnful heap with its gleaming, inspiriting YES. I'm finding this to not be entirely true. These days, instead of turn downs, one should expect...nothing. Stillness, silence, a void in which the query has vanished without ceremony. In my searches, I'm met with a varied repetition of these words: *Do not expect a response. We will reach out if your proposal proves of interest.* Which is worse, I wonder — a blatantly worded sign declaring one's inadequacy or the noiseless cave of The Great Ignore?

On the few occasions an inquiry garnered a response, that hideous ogre, social media, oozed its way into the missive. Not enough to create, no. Not enough to be. I must maintain an online presence; I must be remark(et)able, becoming familiar with demands akin to the following: "*Please describe your platform:* Your platform here is defined broadly as what you bring to the table in marketing your book. It includes your social media network (please include numbers and links), your media history (i.e. print and online coverage, television and radio shows you've been on, etc.) and your real-life network (well-placed individuals who will support your book). Include anything else you feel is relevant to helping us understand how you can help us effectively market your book," I sensed failure loom, dooming my work to the unread pit of the unpublished.

Unwilling to castrate my own dignity, I replied thus: "I am one of those few, and I hope this doesn't disqualify me as an author, who does not use social media or own a smartphone. My real-life network consists of family, friends, and colleagues who appreciate the written word and the humor still to be found in life. Perhaps my very non-platformesqueness could prove a draw as I seem to have become a specimen (or paragon if we want to think more positively about it) of the unplugged. Many find this unique trait compelling, thought provoking, and even praiseworthy. And yes, some don't. May your company exist in the former category."

Sadly, it did not.

I sent the exchange to a friend who acknowledged my lamentable predicament. To this I admitted the concept as a whole is frustrating (and dismaying), but I enjoyed answering in just such a way, even making myself laugh while composing the final sentence. I shared the realization that the only way I could answer the question was to be honest and amuse myself. He again replied, slightly altering my words to express that the only way to respond *to this life* was to be honest and amuse oneself.

Agreed.

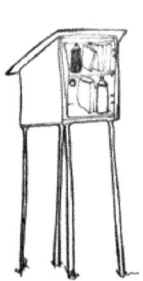

II. ministry of the exterior

What is it that compels so many male hands to etch a representation of the dick on all available surfaces? Following the discovery of yet another penciled penis on the inside cover of a school textbook, I decided to consult the experts, though I used somewhat more genteel language in the asking. With six classes of 10th and 11th graders, my control group lacked large numbers but still provided a sufficient quantity for potential insight. Unfortunately none of their responses ("because you're not supposed to," "nothing better to do," "why not?") convinced. Nor did "It's funny." I don't think so. *Why* is it funny? Again no satisfactory feedback. The fixation simply *must* go deeper than that.

Turning my attention to the females of the group (though the initial question had been posed to the entire class), I confessed, "I've never just *had* to draw a vagina on something. Have you?" Resounding negatives.

Since our discussion delivered little other than pleasure in my oh so obvious consternation, I left them with a newly unbuttoned idea. "Such drawings are so commonplace, it's not as if it really proves anything or makes any sort of statement. I want us to try a new trend. When you finish your assignment today, before turning it in, try drawing other — non-sexual — body parts on your work." We held a brief practice session on the whiteboard. Noses, ears, elbows, ankles, toes, and eyebrows filled the blank space. Leafing through their work, I was met with fingernails, hair partings, cheeks (the facial sort), eyes, knees, and calves. I still receive the occasional note or assignment with belly buttons, thumbs, shoulders, and armpits sketched in the margins. While these sporadic reminders of my positive impact on the youth of America whiffs faintly of optimism, my guidance rests thwarted until the day I drive by a billboard, not defaced but faced (as I like to think of it), with a lung, upper lip, or bicep. Only then shall I solemnly intone, "I have slain my Goliath."

But body parts. How they are obsessed over, ogled, both managed and micromanaged. Breasts, for example, cast a spell I fail to fathom, though of course I agree their twinned health remains paramount (and ought not there exist a lingerie line bearing such a formidable moniker?). Still, I am a new entrant into the world of mammography, only two visitations to boast of in my middled age. Despite being such a novice in boobsquishery, I can't imagine my latest technician earned her merit badge in How to Talk Appropriately to the Patient. Upon gown removal, she scrutinized my form before brightly announcing, "We're going to use the itty-bitty one for you!"

Now I love my breasts, or rather lack thereof. Flatness, except in tires or yeast breads, has never suggested anything but approval in my eyes. For some patients, however, I imagine pause (pained pause) would result from such an assessment. This reminds me of an old joke of a fantasy I conjured in younger years. A favorite daydream involved a visit to a plastic surgeon's office. With a straight face I would request breast reduction surgery "…it hurts to exercise, my back is always sore, I'm worried about the results of aging." I could never do it, of course. Less than skillful with deadpannery am I. But still, what would the doctor say? Would tact be involved? Honesty? Indulgence in the playful farce?

Alighting in the present, cold and clamped existence, I am excused. I exchange the horrid gown for the temporarily abandoned garments of the locker, blessing their familiarity and warmth, their embrasure and love of my very itty-bittiness. I depart the office, corduroys singing their walking song and, as I pass a small pond, the frog chorus silences at the nearest whisper of my approach. A conductor with a mighty baton. With hues of cattails, of autumn leaves abounding, my thoughts turn to paint chips, to naming color. I'd like that job, I think. Among the yellows Butterscotch Frenzy and Midas's Bane. Is spray paint likewise deliciously described? Would I find the color of my winter paled body among its compressed offerings?

Would I — maybe — return to the office to leave a (yes, tiny) mark of my glorious, treasured chest at the base of the building? I smile, but am gratified that still, I fail to understand that particular compulsion.

III. octopi wall street

My friend's daughter committed mass pescicide recently. Wanting to be helpful, she took it upon herself to clean the fish tank. "Clean" meaning pouring soap in the aquarium and rubbing it against the glass walls. Instead of clear waters and unobstructed views of the happy creatures within, she found her little finned friends sleeping with the bubbles.

This brings to mind another unfortunate tale of premature pet demise. I'm sure the misfortunes of hamsters and gerbils the world round are abundant and often gory, but I've never heard one quite like this. My best friend in high school, the oldest of seven children, told me of Hammie III's death. Her youngest sister, perhaps forgetting his presence as her accompanist at the piano, slammed the keyboard lid shut following her performance. No applause erupted, only the death rattle of the hamster. Visiting their house months later, still mourning the loss, she confided in me regarding this continued woe. Expressions of sincere sympathy must have impacted the child. "Would you like to see him?" she asked.

I didn't quite understand. A picture?

"He's in the freezer." Dragging a chair to the kitchen, she clambered up, retrieving a box nestled between the Cookies 'n Cream and frozen peas. It required considerable effort not to laugh at such an encore. The creature, on its back, arms rising straight in front like some horrific parody of a mummy, though thankfully (though maybe not, considering its proximity to the family's sustenance) unswaddled in miniature bandages.

"Why is he still in the freezer?"

With great solemnity, "We're waiting for the ground to soften."

It was July.

Another July, years later, finds me dwelling upon a certain other, more significant (sorry, frozen Hammie) departed soul — my piano teacher and next door neighbor during the fraught teenage years. An intriguing figure six and a half feet tall, wiry of build and Einstein of hair, an accent bearing traces of his Lithuanian background, devotee of Flora, his skittish, piano-hating dog, and accomplished pianist himself. His presence will remain forever fixed in some nook of my mind, partly due to a certain habit I've maintained for the last two decades. In order not to lose my (dubious) ability to play the piano, my hands stutter through at least (*least* being the operative word here) one song a day on the electric keyboard. A limited repertoire is mine and often I turn to the same pages as my youthful, better-sighted eyes beheld propped on the family's upright Baldwin. Giving distinction to so many of these pieces, the faint phantoms of his penciled scrawl drifting through the score. At the time, noting his scribbled reminders, I could not have imagined the middle-aged me fondly remembering this patient musical guide as I return to those familiar notes and melodies. He was my teacher and I was his dog sitter. When I moved away we became, surprisingly, pen pals until his kind and beautiful heart ceased to function, bringing me to that summer years after his death. As a fatherless daughter myself, I reflected that a newly discovered stack of letters written in my own father's robust hand would prove overwhelming. After learning her contact information, I emailed his surviving daughter to ask if she would like the correspondence I'd accumulated.

Yes.

Before sending them to their more rightful owner, I reread his words, ordering them chronologically. His thoughts on television shows, movies, concerts, visits with his granddaughter, politics, and Seattle flowed again before me. A passage about Flora's death ached from the page. He had already lost a wife, a daughter. He wrote he thought he could no longer experience grief but this slight, timid creature of indeterminate breed departed his life, creating yet another trench of loneliness, of sadness, in his already scarred existence.

Preparing the packet, I notice a curiosity on the reverse side of the postcards included: "Space Below is Reserved for the U.S. Postal Service." How nice, I thought, it would be to find a postal worker's added message in that space, a finishing grace note. I muse, cross-legged on the floor, near the sheet music spilling from the wooden milk crates beside the keyboard, awaiting my dexterous fingers. There I go lying again, remembering how my teacher referred to them as "the poor little babies" as in, "Oh, can the poor little babies manage that?" We spent much time working out alternatives to the suggested fingerings of the scores. Among them exists a certain collection of Bach, the cover showing the absolute worst (I certainly *hope* it's the worst, I mean otherwise: poor guy, but then he's Bach so maybe I needn't feel too bad about his face given his other attributes) picture of him gazing outward. Despite its hideousness, I often found myself studying it, trying to imagine what this bloated, bewigged, beloved composer was thinking. One year I decided to bring it to school and hold a caption contest.

I set Johann on the whiteboard tray, allowing him to inspect the students in a manner I'm certain they found unsettling. Participation in the contest was voluntary. I simply explained the requirements and set out a suggestion box…err…Bachs. I so wish I'd taken the trouble to note the best entries received but I can find no record of this vast contribution to the annals of pedagogy, though I certainly remember the winner, for I Sharpied a thought bubble over the bulbous figure and now, whenever I select this book from the others I know his sentiments exactly: "I wish they'd warn you about the after-effects of a colonoscopy."

Oh, Death, I think, addressing the oversized envelope, the

dead composer, you take from us our loves and our lives, coming for us all. From the soap-poisoned fishes to the piano-pummeled rodent...to you...to me.

IV. celebrations are inconvenient

The date was blind. No, let me say the fellow himself boasted sightful eyes; we'd just never met. I fully own this as a character flaw, but my first reaction to a creature of the opposite sex tells me if a spark is there to be kindled or I'm standing before a dud match, impossible to inflame.

The knock came, I opened the door, and before me stood a perfectly decent looking, well-built man, but any potential ardor was instantly snuffed. Not being someone capable of tolerating wasted time, I began planning immediately. Just how much did I owe someone who traveled a considerable distance to meet me? More than five minutes for sure. Even an hour would be pretty skimpy. Two? Could two be enough?

We ambled through a lovely nearby arboretum, I trying to maintain a friendliness limned with asexuality (a delicate balance given my so prominent allure), while he acted the part of a wooing admirer. I wanted to say, "Listen buddy — the charm is lost on me. Let's just take a pleasant stroll so you can stretch those limbs before I fold you back into that rental car and send you on your way." I did not.

Returning to my apartment, I could stand it no longer. As easefully as possible I thanked him for making the effort but confessed I didn't feel our meeting would lead to anything. Oh but he was shocked, showing how completely he believed in the prowess of his courting. He asked to use the restroom, I think more to compose himself than anything, and when he returned, still with a look of baffled incomprehension, requested a cup of tea. Feeling I could spare the time to prepare and watch him sip — really the least I could do — I acquiesced, but I'm no tea drinker. Apologies to those who love the beverage, but I'd rather drink the dregs of my great-aunt's chamber pot. Opening the cupboard I did find two boxes: Good Earth (the most non-tea tea I've ever encountered, and therefore, tolerable) and, given certain times when digestion does not occur like a newly batteried digital clock, Smooth Move. He stood gazing (no doubt longingly, wistfully) through the window, thus missing the visage of a woman thrilling with mirth at the prospect of offering up a mugful of bowel propellant.

I imagine no shock will register over my continued state of singledom despite the passing years (and years (and years)) — the lone suitcase sedately revolving on the baggage carousel — no ring for me. Yes, such imagery rings a muffled bell. The one that got away? Really, I must be an overachiever. Streams of lost men pass before my mind's eye. Okay, trickling streams…streams that dry up frequently and for prolonged periods. Here I feel the need to clarify. I *like* being single and, as I've admitted before, children were never something I wanted in this life. I hear there are others like me, but I don't know them so it still feels a bit of an aberrant state, one in which others do not wish to abide.

So alien is the notion of emigrating from this particular zip code, I stand astonished whenever an exit visa is mentioned. I suppose he's required to pose the question, but I do wonder as my age climbs in elevation, when will it stop? My yearly endocrinology appointment always ends the same way. "Any plans to get pregnant?" Even though this has become a tradition, I block it out somehow, meeting the query with renewed surprise, an inelegant guffaw (though perhaps inelegant rests redundant when describing a guffaw), followed by a blurty "No!" He then asks if I am sure. Sure as a lactose intolerant vegan in an ice cream shop choosing the only nondairy option, Doc.

Leaving my latest adventure in thyroid counts and medication review, I consider all the parties I don't get, being an old(ish) maid of barren womb. Of course, I don't like parties of any kind so if ever I embrace betrothal or pregnancy, I most likely would skip the showers, my own wedding if possible. But simply because I'm enshrouded in seclusion does not dictate ineligibility from the kingdom of kitchen accoutrements, immaculate sheet sets, matching towels, a nifty vase (or two). Then again, maybe it does, given the unwelcome mat predominating my predilections regarding both attendance and hostdom.

A couple years ago, conversing with my brother, he mentioned all the work functions he felt obligated to attend, ending with the statement "Celebrations are inconvenient." A universal truth? Probably not, but if more of us faced our feelings honestly, I would venture, conservatively, half the attendees of most gatherings would rather be elsewhere. I made him a t-shirt with his refreshingly frank confession printed boldly across the chest. An idea: Make many of these in varying colors and fonts. Send them in lieu of RSVPs.

V. preferred doneness

There's a healthy distinction to be made between satisfactions and obsessions. For fun and pleasure's sake, let us devote some time to the former category, straying from the world of uncontrollable compulsions. I'll start with my friend Danielle. We first met at the refreshingly agreeable age of thirteen. A few years into our relationship she shared with me her love of Small Heavy Things. She had, in fact, a small Small Heavy Things collection comprised of dense objects weighing down her hand, the less palm space covered the better. I've surprised her over the years — in person when that's a possibility or in the mail — with miniscule hefties. Sometimes I find them in the street, sometimes they are bits broken off of Large Heavy Things: metal scraps, gobbets of iron, certain rocks even qualify.

I'd like to ask about your own odd delights, but perhaps just a few more examples are necessary before I pose that integral question. It's not quite universal — I know because of the data I've collected by offering pieces of the bubble wrap to students for such accomplishments as composing excellent vocabulary sentences, creating perfect citations, earning a good score on a quiz, or in celebration of their birthdays, but most people do relish the sensation of such popdom. Did the inventor of these air-plumped sheets know they were creating not only an effective wrapping for the shipping of delicate items (albeit environmentally unfriendly) as well as a terrifically gratifying tactile activity (tactivity)? Further research is required.

Yes, I am among the number who takes pleasure in the above, but I find my mind drifting toward more personalized joys. I'm not sure why, but my nine-year-old self really *really* wanted a wastebasket so that's what I asked my paternal grandparents for Christmas. Arnold Sylvester and Norma Bedelia (can you believe those names?! On the satisfaction theme my grandpa had a brother called Hartvig Parelius — now that's just divine to say!) ceased to exist in the physical sense long ago but I wish I could ask their thoughts regarding such a merry request. Whatever their sentiments they obliged and oh my — how blissful a sensation to unwrap a wastebasket, ball up the paper, and toss it in the very receptacle it so recently obscured. Perfection.

Another little treat, and perhaps more than I savor such a discovery...there's something inexplicably wonderful in discovering one's Reese's Peanut Butter Cup (full-sized or miniature) bundled in not one, but *two* frilly little brown papers. A bonus gift, possibly transmitting the message that this particular sweet is a doubly worthy friend of the taste buds.

I also experienced satisfaction phases. For a couple of years in my mid-twenties, I derived exquisite fulfillment in composing and sending peculiar business letters. I believe my two favorites from this personal epistolary era include a dispatch regarding a woodland animal candle set and the initial communication regarding the masculinity quotient inherent in yogurt eating (with a follow up to a different yogurt company which geared their creamy concoctions to men).

First the candles. I saw them in a catalog, disbelief at the sight my primary reaction. Just who (who the *hell*) decided it would be a good idea to offer consumers the unique opportunity to light cute little animals' heads afire? I ended up writing the store (and later their parent company when, strangely, I received no response) after acquiring the candles myself through a curious route. Allow me to map out those circumstances. I showed the ad to a good friend and colleague. We commiserated regarding the utter wrongness of the product. Upon returning from winter break she offered a regift — a present received from her mother-in-law in honor of the holiday celebrating the birth of Christ. Yes, she had been given the flammable set of adorables. This was too much. It was also too much having them look at me in sweet innocence with the omen of imminent destruction jutting from above their blissfully ignorant countenances. I'm not a girl given to leaving items unused so yes, I lit them.

I witnessed wax tears dripping from their doleful eyes, faces melting and, in the end, the squirrel was left completely decapitated, a sad little wick protruding from its neck. Would it haunt me, this charred nut gatherer? Throw a baby pumpkin at my own cowering dome next Hallow's Eve à la the Headless Horsemen and the hapless Ichabod? "Really?" I wrote. "Really? This is what you're comfortable selling? Don't you realize homicidal maniacs frequently begin their bloody exploits with the torture of small animals? What pernicious path are you setting us upon?" Apparently my letter did nothing to open their eyes to product misplacement or any semblance of social responsibility (not to mention taste) on their part. The next year they carried the same set of candles...offered in a larger size.

My first yogurty letter found me adopting an alternate personality, that of a middle-aged man not quite secure enough in his masculinity to eat a cup of live and active cultures in public, regardless of the probiotically charged health benefits. Rather than live a closeted life, he/I suggested beginning a line of products intended for men. Bold colors, manly logos, more robust flavors would set it apart making it, perhaps not as brawny an undertaking as swigging a beer, biting off 1/3 a stick of beef jerky, or spitting tobacco juice while aiming an ax at a seemingly unfellable tree, but less fraught than spooning a bit of lemon chiffon fat free into one's craw at break time.

I often use my documents as examples of the business letter format when instructing students in the rudiments of such — both to (maybe) attract their interest and to (maybe) show another version of fun to these (mostly) uncreative developing beings. A year following such a lesson, a clutch of students from those classes arrived with the exciting news (and ad to prove it) that a new company marketing yogurt for men had indeed been founded. Again I squeezed the fruit of creation, allowing the juice to flavor yet another letter. In this message, I reverted to my female state and confessed to inadvertently eating their product. I further wrote of the anxiety this accidental ingestion caused. What made their products for men? Was I in danger of developing certain unwanted secondary sexual characteristics such as a lowering of the voice, an increase in body hair? Would I suddenly morph into an ardent fan of the Patriots or exhibit a penchant for tugging/adjusting certain areas of my nether regions in full view of others? These were valid concerns.

My business letter stage lessened, eventually vanishing altogether, much to the relief of those in charge of handling corporate correspondence, I imagine. Although it is possible those offbeat and semi-insane communications invigorated the reading life of what could often prove a dull occupation. I like to think so anyway.

Solace in small but heavily important things continues. In a country replete with missing posters for such qualities as morality, intelligence, sanity, selflessness, hope, and optimism, where so many belong to the demographic of The Stupid and The Angry, I shall risk morphing into a reincarnation of Julie Andrews during a thunderstorm with abundant offerings of favorite things, among them: 1. Attempting to meditate while visualizing a "You are Here" sign. 2. Witnessing a covey of quail skittering by in their insistent forward tilt. 3. Noticing the particularites of a fence seemingly fashioned from a giant's discarded Popsicle sticks, wondering what monstrous icy treats once climbed their heights. 4. The moon, a glowing buoy riding the clouds. 5. A young girl, puffed pigtails sprouting from the sides of her scalp like pom-poms celebrating her thoughts. 6. White blossoms forming daylight constellations in dark green shrubbery. 7. The more cheerfully toned Morse code messages of glitter-crowned hummingbirds. 8. The delicate bravery of the fishbone.

But back to you. I have now heaped your plate with examples, desiring the dish be absent any metaphorical parsley.

May they inspire your own mood menders, allowing you to surface from the ugliness sowing this land they deem to be their land (though not too swiftly, thus avoiding the soul's version of the bends — forgetting to care in the midst of such despair).

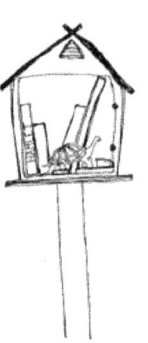

VI. the first option

The term conversation pit does not bode well for the repartee that may occur within its depths, but that, I fear, is where our nation's facility with language exists today. Call me biased, but I'm going to place the blame on smartphones. A tool supposedly designed to promote communication and meaningful exchange has mutated into something else entirely. Venturing seemingly anywhere one witnesses the addicts taking hits from their devices, overdosing on useless information, mindless entertainment, distraction from reality. Okay, okay, all those things have existed in various forms through the centuries and even, I feel, have their place…in demitasse-sized servings rather than brimful troughs of styrofoam. I am biased; I am distraught; I understand if you despise my Ludditical beliefs.

I am also a hypocrite.

I use FaceTime on my computer and I love communicating with my beloved and geographically diffuse family in this manner. I distract myself with the superfluous on this same screen and could certainly abandon many time-wasting pursuits. And yet, I do not place myself among those requiring intervention. I own a flip phone. Based on the self-loathing experienced when I finally made the transition from landline to cellfishness, may its life prove long and indestructible.

This past year, when the students in one class learned I am both smartphoneless and likely to leave my flip phone unpowered for days at a time, such lifestyle choices were met with true incomprehension. One particularly troubled girl struggled to pose her question: "But what if…what if someone's trying to get ahold of you? For an appointment or something?" My response of "They don't" clearly didn't register. Another student wanted to know, "What do you… *do*?" I'll admit many would find my life a cesspit of loneliness and boredom, but I love it (apart from the current political and environmental climate, the overuse of terms like "literally" and "100%," the existence and use of leaf blowers). I read. I walk. I think. I create. I connect. I disconnect. I immerse myself in independent subtlety. Being constantly available is not one of life's essentials. A graph à la the now defunct food pyramid now constructs itself (sans slave labor) in my brain — the "use sparingly" portion reserved for screens and access. There's nothing wrong with obscurity, with privacy. Making a splash is often seen as a good thing but not in diving itself. Are we to take from this a lesson in humility, grace, and inconspicuousness?

Back to the origins of this essay — that pit. Language and expression, though so often woefully inadequate, can extend beyond the heights of precision and beauty. Which brings me to a much needed acronym: TMM (Too Many Montages) included in movie ratings. Soon, I worry, films will consist solely of montages. No dialogue. Is talking so hard? Apparently. The montage says to me this, and nothing else: We didn't have the budget for talented writers or a quality script.

Beyond the montage dwells a different aspect of music in the movies. I find myself mesmerized by the melodically themed subtitles of foreign films and shows, the words chosen to translate the offerings of the soundtrack. Such descriptions as uncanny music, bouncy music, perplexed music, commanding and/or resolute music border the screen. Perplexed? I find the terms concurrently incredibly funny and wildly inaccurate. I'm also curious about the writers of such descriptors. How is it decided that some music is dramatic, very dramatic, or intensely dramatic? I imagine heated debates arising over such gradations as eerie, spooky, bizarre, and mysterious. Does it ever come to blows? And if so, are they regular blows or powerful blows?

My own life's perplexed soundtrack resumed upon returning to the gym following a nearly two year pandemic-sponsored hiatus. Perusing such enlightened publications as

People and *Us* ceased during this span but again diverted my attention from the reality of indoor sweat sessions. Back on the elliptical and flipping through pages, I espied a celebrity (I won't name) and his wife posing for a selfie (selfies?) in Italy, their sideways smooch captured by phone, his eyes directed toward the lens. I couldn't help but feel unsettled (my inner subtitler now stressing over the aptest adverb to describe such inner turbulence). No love or even affection apparent unless, of course, for the imagined vision of his appearance in the photo.

I recall a line from *Mr. Deeds Goes to Town* — a film thankfully rendered in black and white, not with added color, unwholesome-looking, like so many processed foods. At one point, Jean Arthur's character comments, "Too busy in a crazy competition for nothing." Is that what our world has become? Or maybe it's always been so, only the medium varying over time.

I've admitted my own hypocrisy in this arena; I will also

confess to a lack of eloquence under certain circumstances — for instance, when buying underwear from a student. Allow me to explain. Holding a soon to expire coupon from a certain, less than exalted department store, I headed there, heedful of the expiration date. For me such endeavors rank roughly equal with flossing post corn on the cob consumption (two ears: conspicuous consumption). Taking my place in line, I surveyed the cashiers. Often, I liken my brain to a three-way bulb. Observing the staff member most likely to ring up my purchase (two pairs of sensible though pleasantly patterned bikini cut briefs — never have my cheeks been torn asunder by a thong, nor will they ever be), the mind switched to the dimmer setting.

No. Not him. He who once sat amidst a sea of sophomores in my classroom would soon be handling my undergarments. My turn came. I stepped up to the counter. "So here I am. Buying underwear." He nodded. What more could we say? Embarrassingly blushworthy on both our parts yes, but neither of us retreated into the catered world of technological oblivion, escaping this odd connection, this part of shared humanity so many wish to obliterate.

Let us stop such eradication, such customizing of our lives through variously calibrated filters. I refuse to shake the Etch a Sketch of myself, erasing perceived imperfections, the very symbols of living. I hunger for existence rather than portrayal. We are not, nor should we be, Photopshopped versions of ourselves. Yes, we are blessed with opposable thumbs, but that does not necessitate using them to manipulate our beings, to escape from ourselves, from each other, from this wildly diverse and confusing reality.

Undies in backpack (no plastic bag for me), I cross the parking lot under a darkening sky, drinking in that delicious goblet of a view. The moon is in its awkward phase, a malformed marshmallow, but I have no desire to wish it into fullness.

Contented music. Wholly contented music.

VII. limited means

The town of my childhood expanded rapidly. Many of its developments were geared toward the middle and upper-class, but a select few, those called The Street of Dreams, focused solely on those multi-millionaires willing to live in the area or the multi-multi-millionaires in need of a cush second (or third or fourth) house. If by street the name meant many streets and a plethora of cul-de-sacs, and if by dreams the name signified a phantasmagoria of colossal kitchens, multiple master and (misses) suites, boutique-like closets, guest rooms the size of small apartments — big enough to swing several litters of cats (because that's what people like to do in rooms: swing cats) — the title of such developments proved accurate. Living near but not *in* these enclaves of affluence, I developed a warped sense of the essentials inherent in living a happy life. When a new field of homes blossomed forth in gaudy abundance, tours were held affording access to that forbidden, enticing garden. I longed for bathtubs like swimming pools, swimming pools belonging to resort hotels, acres of lawn, and thousands of square footage through which to wander. One model home boasted a children's bedroom painted in such a style the occupant appeared to be forever floating in a hot air balloon basket with views of stunning countryside beauty and other skyriding galleons glimpsable between the ropes and weavings. If I lived in this room, I knew, all life's troubles and all my own flaws would diminish into nothingness.

Why couldn't Mom and Dad be rich? Well, a nurse and a pastor sure couldn't purchase such a domicile, nor would they have wanted to, growing increasingly dismayed with the town's gaze fixing ever so firmly on the extravagant as the *only* existence worthy of pursuit. This is not to say we lived a spartan lifestyle. We had a nice home, owned two cars, never went hungry, spent money on the dog ophthalmologist when our beloved Samoyed, Nicholas, developed glaucoma, took family trips. But did my parents tithe? They did. Did they become foster parents to a brother and sister in need of a home? Indeed. Did Dad forego a drive-thru meal due to a dime dropped between the placing of his order and its pick up? Yes. Their beliefs, their charity and generosity did nothing to quell my avarice for unreal estate. Only age and painful experience upon experience could drain that abscess of excess — disappointment in things, in experiences I ardently believed would cure all life's injuries the only lance powerful enough to penetrate and dispel such convictions.

At some point during this educational process of growing up, my parents' bedroom provided refuge from the torments outside its confines. Their own closet, nothing like the vast bastions of haute couture across town, offered solace. Their mingled senses imbued me with a sense of comfort and safety, the familiar shoes and sweaters, the long skirts which brushed my face as I pushed them apart to sit behind their soft folds, loose hangers jangling. Time spent cross-legged in the darkness varied, but my small form always exited the dim cubby at least partially restored.

No, our house would never be part of a tour, never inspire fascination in its opulence, but here I was loved and accepted with a love and acceptance beyond any I could find elsewhere. A great welcome mat of a home, rooms blooming into being by lamplight wherein dwelled the reliables of life: my mom and dad, my brothers, each of us seeking and finding repose in our modest, plainly painted bedrooms.

And back to the supposed panacea of that other chamber. I recently read a newspaper account detailing the horrors of a hot air balloon tragedy. Insensitivity to the suffering of others replaced the sickness with which I read the story. I realized that envious longing for wealth, the charm of eternal balloon-basket living was now forever destroyed. Adding further evidence to the bounteous case of solipsism (there may be no "i" in team, but there are no less than three in that syndrome), a fire from my past rekindles.

Ice storm '96. Until the city froze and blacked out, I didn't even know such a phenomenon existed. Like certain things in life it was utterly beautiful and utterly hazardous simultaneously. Schools shut down, driving became nearly impossible, the power went out — our house's for eight days. The cold seeped into everything. I honestly can't recall what we ate or how we dealt with so many of the daily practicalities of life, though I do remember candlelit games as one entertainment, a certain one in particular. I enjoy a rousing round of Scrabble at any time and its sustaining power surpasses even the coldest and darkest of conditions.

I formed my first romantic alliance as a senior in high school. Though I loved him in that deep end, first love manner, he morphed into the most deviant of rivals when sitting across that board with his seven tiles and rapidly configuring mind. We sat on the floor, candles to the side, eyes riveted to the burgeoning crosshatch of words before us. So enrapt with our letters and the addictive power of wordy prowess, we failed to notice in our intensity his shirt caught fire. Perhaps a differing pattern of glimmer caused me to look up and when I did, suddenly all those fire safety elementary school assemblies rushed over me. In a jubilation of rote-learning, I yelled. "Get on the ground and roll!"

He did as I bade, extinguishing himself while burning multiple holes across the length of the family room carpet. Apparently the premium for boyfriend burns sustained during a not so friendly clash of the tiles subsequently causing damage to the home was met and an insurance check to cover the damage arrived. The pre-scorched carpet had long needed replacing, but given our previously mentioned pecuniary state, we could not afford such a luxury.

I would call it a win-win-win situation. He survived, a new and upgraded floor covering would soon buffer our steps, I won. Or did I? Of all the mysteries here related, the one troubling me the most at the moment: How can I not remember if we finished the game? And if so, did I allow a triple word score for such an incendiary play?

I still own that Scrabble board. Patiently it rests upon a shelf in a small, non-Street of Dreams sized closet, wax globules spotting the board, capable of eliciting a veritable cosmos of memory.

VIII. nice threads

I first learned how in my teenage years but didn't fully embrace and revel in the art until my twenties. It has since become an integral part of my identity and sense of fulfillment. The question to ask yourself at this point in the paragraph: What is she talking about? Were this an interactive page, I would be curious to read some responses, but as that is beyond my limited technological capacities, I will simply acknowledge I am writing of my hobby, my art, my cloth and thread fascination — cross-stitch. I discovered early on that following *all* the directions would be neither enjoyable nor sustainable. Certainly the pictures themselves needed no improvement, but the prepared sayings called for my own particular brand of refinement.

It all started with my brother Andrew. Toiling through his Ph.D program, he shared the working title of his dissertation, a caption from the cover of *Time* magazine. I loved it immediately in all its truthful pessimism: "Man's story is not a success story." Knowing I needed a special gift with which to mark the completion of his work and entry into the world of titled doctordom, I found a cross-stitch pattern of bluebirds and flowers. The message should have been "Welcome to the Andersons' (or Smiths' or Pemrokes'), but I stitched in the quote — it turns out inaccurately — placing the apostrophe in the wrong place, though I suppose my error more appropriately embodies the statement's theme. This masterpiece (flawed masterpiece, okaypiece?) now graces Dr. Andrew's desk. Thus marks the beginning of my needled career.

I sometimes wonder how I could possibly spend so many of the precious hours of this life fashioning these works. Most take months to complete and I have given all but one away. I do spend more time enjoying my other favorite pastimes — reading and moving my body — but cross-stitch lends itself to a particular form of multitasking. I can listen to podcasts or visit with others, either on FaceTime or in person, leaving me feeling instructed, entertained, or sociable while still productive. And there are different levels of pleasure involved in the stitching. When the picture first begins to emerge as something more than blocks of colored squares, a subtle happiness emerges with the newly visible image. The more intense joy comes with the creation of the caption. Sometimes I know it before even puncturing the cloth, at others midwork, and still others upon tying up the final piece of thread. When just the right words arrive — usually funny and nearly always filthy — the elation of comedic innovation festoons my soul. Sharing these works with others and hearing their reactions (of course the offerings reach an edited audience — among others, Aunt Carol must be sheltered from certain aspects of my personality) adds that extra dollop of delight to the venture.

Why do I love inappropriateness so much, even if I'm careful (most of the time) to avoid it in life? It generally, thankfully, remains locked within where I can freely revel in all the wonderful, awful possibilities for it we are afforded each day. I've always cherished Quint from the movie *Jaws*, perhaps because he doesn't limit this world to his mind. My favorite toast (ever) occurs aboard the *Orca*, that too small boat. Imbibing freely while sharing scars accrued through the years, he raises a glass: "Here's to swimmin' with bowlegged women!" Knowing full well he would love it but could never (for good reason!) wear it in public, I found a Quint t-shirt echoing this gem for my oldest brother's birthday.

*Side note: Can I here make a joke about my own mother's bowleggedness on this halcyon birth day? Presumably not.

*Center note: I invented a game: worst places to don such a garment. Open house at school? A triathlon? A friend emerged triumphant with the suggestion of a Me Too Rally.

While I have no problem with Quint and his bawdy, bullying personality, when Pipet dies while playing fetch in the waves pre-Alex Kintner's evisceration, now that offends. This makes no sense for, in real life, I view the bawdy bully as the acme of opprobrium, a bile-spewing excrescence. But then, the things I don't know could fill an encyclopedia set entitled *Things Katherine Finstuen Does Not Know: Part I*. Entries could include any of the following. Why am I so grossed out by the spellings of "foetus" and "yoghurt" when their close companions do not compel the desire to disgorge my very well-balanced breakfast? Who thought a vacuum of untapped innovation existed before the advent of wax museum torture chambers? I still haven't recovered from a childhood tour of the dastardliness humans have devised in inflicting pain on others, as rendered by agonized figures undergoing such visionary demolition. Why are people described as having two left feet but never two left hands? When it comes to juggling, I'm a definite double-lefty. And why aren't those blessed with my name called Erin for short? Yet it's still there, this ardor for the unseemly, I realize with the rude awakening of feet recently fallen asleep. When my brain does its terrible thing and the devil hitching a ride on one shoulder takes over, I know which ancient mariner I want to raise a glass with: the obscene one. Admittedly, while the former wandered the world in interminable atonement, the latter found his fate being slowly digested in the belly of the enemy. Does my brain belong there too?

Orca interior. Late at night. Cable knit sweaters abody, strong liquor at hand. "Did I tell you about my last gynecological procedure? Yeah, the doctor squirted vinegar up there. Added a camera to the mix so I could view the whole indecent exposure on the big screen. Afterwards, a bit bandy-legged myself, found relief in the toilet. Turns out I really *am* full of piss and vinegar."

Nah, that one's not so bad. Not quite Quint worthy — that would include bottling my essence as a gourmet dressing in single use plastic to be drizzled over unsustainably farmed seafood — but still too much for my aunt. I suppose what I should take from this is a ride on the metaphorical see-saw of my mental playground. The rise and fall is certainly entertaining, but a place, too, exists for balance. Go ahead and sew a darling Dalmation puppy with the caption, "At least you don't clean your ass with your face" or a fun-loving summer soiree of flip-flopped abandon pronouncing the worthy aphorism "Life is better when you're not a fuck face." But maybe temper those with the less improper, though still jaded, seashell collection's advice to "Underestimate the power of positive thinking." And there are times, surely, to produce a collection of sweetly personalized teddy bear Christmas ornaments for the children of friends and family, their names the sole adornment. I envision them, my inner Quint, my inner aunt Carol, in dynamic equilibrium, meeting each other's gazes comfortably and authentically clear-eyed, not quite teetering, not quite tottering.

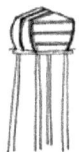

IX. certificate of condemnation

During one of many peaks of the pandemic (that never-ending mountain range of viral eruption), termites continued in their greedy consumption of my condo complex. Though the homeowner's association delayed and delayed, eventually they decided this smorgasbord of architecture may well be reduced to the picked over offerings of any banquet: the crumbs of a cake, the crusty leavings of a casserole, one of the lesser salads — merely the edifice's foundation remaining. The residents must evacuate the premises for several days. In this case, a tent would not offer refuge, but poison, occupants thrust outward until the mite-y had fallen. Now there's never an ideal time to leave one's home, but let's call these circumstances less than auspicious. Where to go? Staying with others invited positive feedback on a test no one wants to take. Hotels offered scant security. Perhaps choosing the greater of two evils, I reached out to my insurance agent. He said I *did* have coverage for lodging, but I first had to file a claim. Thus followed a bizarre telephone conversation; clearly the person with whom I spoke operated strictly from a script with no room for deviation. She needed an exact date when the problem occurred. I explained it takes years for such damage to accrue. She insisted on a single day. Reluctantly, I cited the date of the inspection. I was asked about the weather; I was asked if the authorities were called. I couldn't help but imagine the tiny beasts corralled into the backseat of a cop car manacled with cuffs capable of clasping multiple appendages. She required a specific time for the incident. Again I described the grievous process of deterioration, but she repeated her demand. I confessed I didn't think the termites had set meal times but the inspector arrived at 9:30 a.m. My imagination configured the buggy horde tying minuscule bibs around their necks and sitting down to chomp in this copious breakfast booth of a home. Bon appetit, my wee nemeses. Would you prefer a side of wall or ceiling? A garnish of shelving?

Phone calls and emails ate up my time as the pests persisted in their manifeast destiny. A lengthy debate over terminology ensued: Could they be classified as vermin? If so, hello compensation. If not, seek other accommodations. Due to a severe mid-January storm, I had to pack up seemingly *everything* (those familiar with the process know of the tedium involved) and move out…twice. During the second round of exile, a vacant house owned by a friend's parents became available. Thus, the only "vacation" I experienced in nearly two years involved occupying a home left empty due only to another's medical misfortunes and located twenty minutes up the road. For obvious reasons, I still count myself among the lucky ones during this awful period.

Like so many compatriots, a sense of insurmountable anxiety had taken permanent residence in my psyche several years prior — well before the pandemic. I suppose that particular form of unease could be designated the termites of one's soul. How could I possibly tent it out of my being? I sought ways to lessen its invasive power.

Short meditations, deep breathing, yoga, positive mantras. Somewhere during my explorations, my mother remembered a co-worker from long ago, a woman dedicated to the salutary value of fluffing one's aura. Fluffing? Yes. Apparently like head-flattened pillows, our psyches can become thought-flattened, requiring some puffery. I turned where we often turn these days for increased information — not towards the wisdom of an elder or a call to a psychiatrist, but Google, the storer of simply everything, one gigantic Pyrex dish containing the vast and hearty stew of the universe. I found a YouTube video (of course) in which a woman named Isabel, in heavily accented English, speaks of the aura, how it can jolt out of proper alignment, and what aura handicapped individuals can do to pep theirs up, to revitalize and lighten the density of their energy ("How to Fluff"). This involves a simple rolling motion with the arms and hands moving about in different directions. Given the instructions, concern mounted on behalf of all those one or (no!) armed folks seeking guidance. Fortunately, my bodily construction offered no difficulties. Now I'm not convinced it *did* anything, but there was something soothing in the practice and the term so pleased I couldn't help but share the clip with a select few. My sister-in-law immediately responded with her own video from *Saturday Night Fever,* a dance scene. "Clearly," she wrote, "John Travolta was ahead of his time." She was right. Just watch him twiddle those arms like oversized thumbs and if not already convinced of the great power of personalized atmospheric plumping, you will be.

I moved back in, the interlopers vanquished at last — the termites, that is. Those interior gnawers require a much more complex and arduous system of eradication. I reflect upon this as the kettle boils water for the morning's coffee, my eyes roaming the photos and postcards, the magnets and notes affixed to the refrigerator door, my attention caught by a scrap in my own handwriting. I'd copied it down years before after requesting to be taken off an email list from some religious group or other: "You have been unsubscribed from: inspiration." Why did it amuse me so, this judgment? Eternal damnation, indeed, but an additional living hell of blandness preceding the infernal descent.

Oh, hell. Somehow, I can't recall my father ever mentioning it, whether at home or in his sermons. He felt, rightly so, humans are more than capable of manufacturing their own hells, both for ourselves and others. He couldn't know what truly waited beyond this realm, so did not find cause to worry over it — a good approach, combined with his dedication to the staid power of low expectations. As his own end neared, a phrase uttered by a parishioner folded into these thoughts. The man had expressed gratitude for his ability to sit upright and take nourishment. Dad, a reveler in all life's seemingly small blessings, took great pleasure and comfort in both the phrase and his ability to do so until the end. I think about this frequently. What a wonder! I can do that; I can sit upright and take nourishment, even on my lowest days (and there are many). Imagine the consumption of soup, not to mention cereal, without this daily gift.

While the exterminators deprived the termites of this beautiful boast, it will take time and effort, depth of thought, and dedication to goodness to impede anxiety and despair, along with their avatars, from consuming my well-being. Rather than give in, joining the ranks of the sludge-hearted, I will persist with appreciation, curiosity, creativity, and kindness while they stick to a ludicrous script, outdated and ill-informed, benefitting no one but themselves.

I am not unsubscribed from inspiration, no matter what your automatic response says.

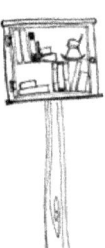

X. double solitaire

As a freshman in high school I started a club: The Anti-Social Club. We never met as that would defeat its purpose. This is true. It is also true, as earlier attested, that retreating into the shut down and isolated world of 2020 did not pose much of a challenge to me. Oh there was stress, fear, sadness, but as for day to day living, spending the majority of my time alone vs. spending the majority of my time alone in a slightly altered fashion could hardly be counted as a burdensome transition.

Work life proved another matter entirely, although some traditions endure regardless of circumstance — such as that barrel of boredom known as the teacher work day preceding the beginning of school. That year it Zoomed into being rather than being held in drafty halls filled with uncomfortable chairs sat upon by staff fueled by unpalatable snacks. During one lengthy spate of screened tedium, the district's nurse provided updates, ending her presentation with a call to look out for those unlucky enough to live alone. Watching out for them, it seemed to her, an altruistic act akin to organ donation, our lives unmatched if not our livers.

The following day, I composed an email, sending it to many of my revered colleagues: "As our nurse so kindly pointed out, there are those among us who are totally alone — childless, partnerless, bereft in this world of social isolation, in need of special consideration and attention in their pathetic solitude — worthy of the charitable attention of those whose life's cornucopia is replete with blessings. Thank you in advance for all your concern."

Oh, the presumptuousness of the phrase "Thank you in advance." If I never see that at the end of an email again I will…I will…send up both prayers and thanks to whichever saint or deity is most closely associated with email composition (surely such an entity exists) *after the fact*. While we're at it, let's get rid of "Best" as a closing sentiment as well. Best what? If you don't have anything but "best" to say, don't say anything at all.

Most of my coworkers understood the satire, though alarmingly, not all. One of the comprehenders more recently observed, "You are the most reclusive person I've ever met." I don't think that's a bad thing. Not really. Many figures I find fascinating would rank in the Olympics of lonerdom. For example (though one might argue he doesn't count because he's animatronic): the rocking chair man espied at the outset of Disneyland's Pirates of the Caribbean ride. His intrigue only grew during the pandemic. Always solo, during the shut down zero visitors placed him farther out of reach than ever, and I simply could not erase him from my mind. He reigned, companionless, upon so much — the pirates, whores, fires, prisoners roiling the watery deep below — calmly rocking aboard his houseboat porch. He remained, I surmised, equally unperturbed as no one passed by in a tourist vessel, turmoil prevailing across the globe. What else occurred in the deserted Disneyland? Was the Haunted House even spookier, or less so, without the witnesses? Could one still wish upon the vapors of bygone firework displays, those dandelion fields of the sky?

Allowing my attention to shift toward the living and breathing, I wonder about the workers deprived of their Disneyfied duties. A certain individual comes to mind. We happened upon her, my companion (eight months pregnant with her first child) and I, several times during that trip, always in the same crosswalk, she heading out as we headed in. Doubtless she worked in food service, some corner of that happy land dedicated to the provision of frosty treats. She wore a dress topped by an apron announcing, above a double scooped graphic: Tasty Cones. If the placement of the words had differed, if she'd been a man instead, I would not have found the sight so arresting, but no. Those letters traced cheerily across her own overflowing cups. Was this a joke? Was this a mistake steeped in extreme density? I could not answer this question but I could, I knew, use the material to my advantage.

Returning home I configured a similar design, ordering a customized apron for my friend and mother to be, her baby shower imminent. Of course, I don't attend such things (refer to essay IV if the mind stumbles), but I would not deprive her of such an inspired offering. I made a delivery of my own — this offspring of ingenuity — to her parents. Thus the gift made it to the shower, my umbrella of protection from such events unfurling sanctuary.

While I do shield myself from much, even finding solo holidays (save one — I've spent two Christmases alone and that is too much of a hermetically sealed existence even for me) offer their own form of celebration. With no need to travel and no engagements, I walk, I think, and I witness in a special brand of seclusion. This last Thanksgiving, my steps covering a lonely, untrafficked road, the reduce speed sign, with nothing else to do, clocked my pace.

The numbers varied between 4-5 miles per hour, yet still

it cautioned me to slow down. No thank you. An anti-social meeting, invitation accepted, awaits, in a vacant rocker that can only be filled by me. I'll give my thanks from this comfortable perch, and punctuality is always appreciated.

XI. in praise of talking to strangers (most of the time)

I never learned to swim. They kicked me out of swimming lessons. Dance class too. My offenses? Refusing to open my eyes underwater. Refusing to perform in a recital. I *liked* the water, I *liked* dancing, but these were the days before everything a child did or did not do merited praise, if not a trophy. Don't fall in line and… you're done. So yes, I spent more time in water wings than a typical child. Sometimes I wish I had them now, though in the metaphorical sense. A pair to help do taxes, to aid in negotiating with difficult people, to provide assistance in the assembly of patio furniture. I like thinking of the patterns I'd choose – Welsh Corgis, Monterey cypress trees, otters (they always look like they're having a good time, save when they're drenched in oil post spill because, well, humans).

Symbolic arm floaties could also help one's spiritual buoyancy when otter thoughts go dark. I suppose memories and favored mind tropes can also serve this purpose. To cheer myself I'll abandon my Eeyore ears of gloom (of course I own a pair) and pull up the inflatable armbands (Brombærsnitter this time — really I just like the word — saw it in a Danish bakery display case) and recall thoughts of uplift. There's my conception of water polo, for one. Awaiting the turn of a traffic light from red to green, I passed the time reading the veritable bulletin board of bumper stickers before me — one of which honored the members of such a team. I saw them in my mind, the players wielding mallets, valiantly straddling their seahorses. A different drive had me relishing the skips of my French language cds. Rather than annoyance, I entertained myself with dreams of speaking French with the same stutter as my disembodied tutor. Thoughts of my father, particularly his idiosyncrasies, likewise bolster. He couldn't lie, that man; therefore, notes written for the attendance office to excuse a tardy so often tended toward the ridiculous. With no good reason for the delayed arrival to school, he once hastily penned a note, handing over a true exemplar of genius: "Katherine is late today…and I know it. -John Finstuen (Father)." Another trait. He thrilled in bad jokes. Sadly for some, this apple of Chelan (my birthplace), fell very close to that tree.

A waitress would ask of his empty plate, "Can I steal that away from you?"

"Yes," he would reply with great inward mirth, "but don't think of it as theft."

One more. He disposed of certain edibles, most notably shelled peanuts at a baseball game, the body of Christ during communion, with an odd and powerful vigor. Of course we made fun of him, my brothers and I: *Dad! You're eating Jesus wrong!* In fact, we worried some Sunday he'd knock himself cold with the force of that palmed wafer. In that same venue we'd snicker over his announcement prevailing the congregation to support the Foss Home Fruitcakes baked goods benefit.

Foss Home was a retirement home.

Think about it.

I suppose it's natural, the making fun of one's parents. If I had children, I know they would have ample stock from which to choose, my tendency to converse with strangers chief among them. If I can forge a meaningful or silly (or if I'm lucky both at one blow) connection, the day's enrichment thermometer reaches lofty heights indeed. The danger exists in choosing wrongly — the wrong person, the wrong approach. Mostly the interactions prove fruitful, beneficial to both parties, but sometimes…sometimes…that same thermometer's measure sinks to levels of abysmal humiliation.

One such dip into cringedom is sponsored by one of my people (one of my former people, that is). I think we all have them — individuals we do not know but who, due to some coincidence of habit or schedule have woven themselves into the pattern of our life. Many representatives of this category can dapple or darken the day. One who dappled journeyed afoot to the local high school while I, unbeknownst to her, embarked on my commute in the other direction (sometimes practicing faulty French). I loved this girl. She exemplified good cheer when my own mood tended toward the opposite end of the spectrum. Quite simply, a day brightener: a smile on the face of the morning. Our "relationship" lasted more than a year, until my big fat mouth intruded. Yes, I saw her in the grocery store one day. Overly excited, I approached, confessing what a wonderful aspect of my daily round she'd proven herself to be, and for so long. Although response was negligible, I did not ascertain just how unwelcome my attentions must have been. No, that insight arose the next morning, the one after that, and the many trailing forever afterwards. No more sightings. That poor girl, forced to change her walking route in avoidance of the crazy lady accosting innocents in pursuit of after school nourishment. Acute awareness of my obtuseness besieged my being.

Yet, if I never dared speak to the unknowns, so much would be missed. On one recent ramble, I paused my steps to speak with a man watering his bounty of a yard just down the street from true majesty. I'd noticed it on many occasions, that swing, affixed by thick cables to the uppermost branches of immense twinned trees. Not wanting or willing to break some privately owned swing ordinance (imagine the consequences of such fun folly), I questioned him. We discussed the wisdom of such a deed. Not a vacant lot, he told me; it hovered so temptingly above privately owned land. "They come around once a year or so. I really don't think they'd mind." After chatting a bit longer, I bade good-bye to John (we were on a first name basis by then). Still uncertain, I decided to wait, a decision that quickly evaporated, the lure of such bait too potent. Climbing a small hill with some trepidation, I glanced about before settling myself in the seat of such glory. And glory it was! The sunshine and windrush, tissue scrap clouds littering the sky, a sprinkling of magnificent minutes seasoning the day.

Hopping back to earth, to reality, I felt the necessity of another set of wings. Periwinkle polka dots this time, with the following message (the script royal blue) serving as a gentle reminder:

Dear Katherine,

Grant yourself the serenity of mind to accept the marvelous connections that can occur between strangers, the courage to understand that not everything needs to be said during such encounters, and the wisdom to know the difference.

Thank you in advance,

Me

XII. purposeful groupings

I'm not a fan of jigsaw puzzles myself, though many of my acquaintance savor the hours spent fitting those mutated amoebae of cardboard together. For many, the more challenging — thousands of pieces, indefinite images — compel a sense of pride upon completion. The other day I amused myself thinking of the worst (to me — difficult to them) puzzle imaginable: one depicting another enormous puzzle as yet unput together. Just as I would find this an unsolvable enigma, I'm baffled by the realization that I have spent nearly half my life in high school. For someone who didn't like it in the first place, I sometimes wonder what sort of masochistic twitch of personality led me to spend so much time there as an adult. From whence was such a motivation dredged? An extra sixteen years crowning the original four! Still, there were aspects of goodness both then and now.

The original quartet left me with a diploma from Lewis

and Clark in Spokane, Washington. I loved the building itself, a mammoth of brick, enormous windows in every aboveground classroom, a veritable art gallery displayed above the lockers, and those heated benches! What divinity to sit upon that ancient wood situated just above a radiator (during the winter months my eyelashes would freeze during the short walk from car to school, melting during first period). This era marked the continued cultivation of my friendship with Danielle, she of the Small Heavy Things collection (see essay V). Demonstrating our devotion to each other, I recall two instances. One of her life's tribulations — differentiating between Vince Lombardi, Guy Lombardo, and Vince Guaraldi — inspired a homemade birthday present: a study guide devoted to outlining their unique qualities. And Danielle, knowing of my longing for glove compartments to accurately reflect their name, stole my gloves, hiding them within my hand-me-down teal Taurus. While sorry to have misplaced them, when eventually I discovered the gloves, their knitted fingers asplay in that coziest of alcoves, it was with the joy that, well, I learned of the following incident during my second high school career.

Class discussion had drifted to the lame gifts we recollected giving our parents during early childhood — ones we'd deemed sublime at the time, but in hindsight, not so much. One girl regaled us with her own contribution. With both parents large animal vets, she often accompanied them on house (or, rather, barn) calls. She grew accustomed to watching her father as he interacted with and healed beasts of all kinds, on numerous occasions witnessing him palpate pregnant cows (she made sure to inform me what this meant as the movie *City Slickers* comprised my entire intelligence of bovine birth). Wanting to make him something truly special to commemorate their time together, she conceived of a project, gathering a Ken doll, a sharpened knife, a cow figurine, glue. I foresaw disaster given the second implement in this gift recipe but no, no children were harmed in the making of this artifact. She simply chopped Ken's hands off at the wrist, glued said wrists to the hindquarters of the animal, and stood back to admire this replica, no doubt lovely in her mind, of her father with his hands up a cow's vagina. Oh but I want to see a) the masterpiece itself b) the way in which the wee girl presented her offering c) her father's face upon the grand unveiling.

Another bauble tinkling from my high school charm bracelet arrived in the form of an email from a student who'd taken a picture of a peer's skateboard. I've seen many skateboards stickered up, expressing bits of the owner's fundamental personality to the world, but never one quite like this. Just one embellishment affixed to the center of the board: my school photo (complete with yearly accessory, a beribboned wand). Before you begin traveling down the thought lane of Look Who Has a Crush on His Teacher, allow me to dispel the notion. This kid could harbor no such feelings for me. I wouldn't let him get away with *anything*, sat him in the very middle of the front row (which he hated), and engaged in the near-constant pursuit of keeping him on task. I was a mosquito in human form — not bloodthirsty, but productivity seeking. When I saw him after receiving the email, I mentioned it, asking, "Does this mean you're somehow fond of me or that you want to stomp on my face?"

Giving his response more consideration than most of the questions posed over the school year, he soberly replied, "Both."

I asked the young man if he loved his skateboard. Without any hesitation he answered "Yes." I then fetched the yearbook photo he (among other students) had tacked onto the classroom wall, cut off the background, and taped it to a possession secured in my wallet. Bringing him the final product, I announced, "I love my library card."

And I do love it, my book passport. Not only it, but the make believe permit with its boundless access to the little free libraries of my neighborhood and the little free library of my mind, a richness of words and ideas, perceptions and memory.

about face

Last summer, following a year-and-a-half of pandemic living sans human touch, sans family, sans a maskless existence, I rejoined the gym, I entered establishments without a face covering, I hugged, I made plans to visit my family — my outlook as if doused in some divine elixir. I do not know why I held such hope for the state of the world. My oldest brother viewed things more realistically and when my mood again peered over the railing of a gloom-filled hollow, he commented, "It's not as if we couldn't see this coming. Yeah, things were improving but then dipshittery takes over." Undeniably. I think our currency should be imprinted with this maxim. Forget E pluribus unum. Dipshittery bespeaks a higher truth. A profound sadness enveloped and in that same sad casing, a belief that humans had inherited exactly what they deserve and the dipshittery shows no sign of waning.

Yet, I should like to close with something more cheerful

than this pandumbic of diseased bodies, diseased minds, diseased morals. I admit a lack of optimism. Although yes, my dearly befuddled — and I include myself in this vast congregation — it is heartening to know so many of us are here to live honestly, authentically, and to somehow find both humor and love in pockets amid such prevailing dissolution. We *can* keep going although in this going we will repeatedly be met with those whose motives and lack of decency defy comprehension. It's hard for me to accept such people exist, but I must — and therein lies one of life's most difficult trials — not only acceptance but a striving to not participate in this hatred of the other.

Segueing inexpertly through the doors of a public restroom stall, ample evidence proves the previous occupant had struggled, desperately, with the toilet seat covers. Have we not all so struggled? Furthermore, have we not all experienced embarrassing moments involving the consumption of cherry tomatoes? Sometimes I find it helpful to focus on what brings us together when so many powers desire nothing more than to cater to (at an outrageous price) the most depraved aspects of our character.

So I continue. Sometimes only barely, at others, exceeding speeds of 4.78 miles per hour.

Katherine Finstuen | 100

Works Cited

"How to Fluff Your Aura (Donna Eden Exercise) - Isabel Martins." *YouTube*, YouTube, 26 Apr. 2017, https://www.youtube.com/watch?v=YkB14eXXzFc&t=7s.

Jaws. Directed by Stephen Spielberg, Universal/Zanuck-Brown, 1975.

Mr. Deeds Goes to Town. Directed by Frank Capra, Columbia Pictures Corp. Presents, 1936.

Time, March 8, 1948, http://content.time.com/time/magazine/0,9263,7601480308,00.html.

www.ingramcontent.com/pod-product-compliance
Lightning Source LLC
Chambersburg PA
CBHW042353070526
44585CB00028B/2911